10 Things Pope Leo XIV Wants You to Know

SR. GEMMA MORATÓ SENDRA, OP

Catholic. Pastoral. Trusted.

Imprimi Potest:
Kevin Zubel, CSsR, Provincial
Denver Province, The Redemptorists

Published by Liguori Publications
Liguori, Missouri 63057

Liguori Publications, a nonprofit corporation, is an apostolate of the Redemptorists (Redemptorists.com).

To order, visit Liguori.org or call 800-325-9521

ISBN 978-0-7648-2898-0
E-ISBN 978-0-7648-7278-5

Printed in the United States of America
29 28 27 26 25 / 5 4 3 2 1

Cover Image: Stefano Spaziani
Pope Leo XIV, visit to the sanctuary of Our Lady of Good Counsel in Genazzano, May 10, 2025.

INTRODUCTION

A New Chapter for the Church

The election of Pope Leo XIV marks a significant turning point in the life of the Church. At a time when the world is grappling with division, disillusionment, and rapid change, the Holy Spirit has raised up a shepherd whose life story is quietly revolutionary—marked not by power or prestige but by simplicity, community, and tireless service. Formerly Cardinal Robert Francis Prevost, this humble Augustinian friar from Chicago has stepped into the shoes of the fisherman with a clear message: the Church must return to the heart of the gospel, walk with its people, and witness to the living Christ with courage and compassion.

In a striking contrast to the ceremonial grandeur often associated with a new papacy, Leo XIV's first public appearance was disarming in its simplicity. There were no grand declarations, no theatrical gestures. Instead, there was a quiet reverence, a humble gaze, and a message that was deeply intentional. "Peace be with you," he said—echoing the first words of the risen Christ. And with those words, a tone was set for his entire pontificate: one of peace, humility, fraternity, and mission.

Pope Leo XIV does not see the Church as a fortress to be defended but as a bridge to be built. His Augustinian roots have instilled in him a spirituality that is both contemplative and missionary—a restless search for God that is only fulfilled in community and service. He brings to the papacy a wealth of lived experience: as a missionary in the poor regions of Peru, as a seminary formator, as the superior general of his Order, and as prefect of the Dicastery for Bishops. These roles have not distanced him from the people but have deepened his commitment to walk with them—to listen, to heal, to accompany.

The ten themes in this booklet are drawn

directly from profound reflections on the first days of Pope Leo XIV's pontificate. They are not abstract theological statements, nor are they policy points. They are the fruit of a life rooted in prayer, community, and love for the gospel. They are the compass points of a Church that dares to dream again—of peace, unity, dialogue, and shared discipleship.

This is a pope who believes that holiness is not reserved for the few but is the vocation of all. That the Church must be missionary not only in word but also in action. That synodality is not an option but is a path to rediscovering the face of Christ in one another. That Mary walks with us. And that evil will not have the final word.

As you read these ten themes, allow them to challenge, comfort, and inspire. Because in Leo XIV, the Church has not just found a pope—it has found a fellow pilgrim. One who reminds us, gently but firmly, that the journey of faith is not one we walk alone, but together. In the one Christ, we are one.

1.

Seek God With a Restless Heart

At the core of Pope Leo XIV's spirituality is a profound restlessness—a yearning for God that echoes the famous words of Saint Augustine: "You have made us for yourself, O Lord, and our heart is restless until it rests in you." This phrase is not simply theological poetry for Pope Leo; it is the rhythm of his life and ministry. His journey, from his early days in the minor seminary to the papacy, has been one of continual searching, listening, and responding to God's call, not in isolation but in communion.

Leo XIV is shaped by the Augustinian vision of a communal life in which the search for God is shared, not solitary. From the very beginning, he understood that truth is not reached alone, but in the embrace of fraternity, mutual care, and shared prayer. His formation in the Order of Saint Augustine taught him that contemplation and mission are not separate callings, but two aspects of the same pursuit—an interior life open to God and an outward life poured out in service.

As an Augustinian, Leo XIV does not seek God in abstract doctrines but in lived relationships. He believes that the Christian cannot claim to follow Christ without belonging to the Church. Just as Augustine taught that Christ is the Head of the Church and we are his body, Pope Leo insists that community is not optional for discipleship—it is essential. His life has been shaped by this conviction, leading him to roles that have formed communities of discernment, prayer, and action—from novice master to seminary rector to prior general of his Order.

This restlessness is not a burden but a gift. It has driven Pope Leo to the mission fields of Peru, to the dusty roads of Trujillo, and later to the leadership of the global Augustinian Order. It is a restlessness that seeks to serve rather than to dominate, to listen rather than to declare. In the poor communities of Peru, he found the gospel lived with joy amid suffering, and in the governance of his Order, he learned that authority, when shaped by love, creates communion.

What distinguishes Pope Leo's restlessness is that it does not seek answers for the sake of certainty but for the sake of love. It is a restlessness that pushes the Church beyond complacency and into deeper intimacy with God and solidarity with others. It is not about intellectual control but about humble openness. Like Augustine, Pope Leo believes that God is not a distant reality but the One who is found in shared bread, common questions, and the cry of the poor.

To seek God with a restless heart is to live with longing, humility, and hope. It means refusing to settle for mediocrity and choosing instead the path of inner transformation and outward service. This is the journey Pope Leo invites us to take with him—not toward comfort but toward communion. And it begins, as it did for him, with a restless heart that dares to believe that God is near.

2.

Be Artisans of Peace

When Pope Leo XIV stepped onto the central balcony of Saint Peter's Basilica for his first public appearance, the words he chose were not political, nor poetic, nor strategic. They were gospel: "Peace be with you." These same words were spoken by the risen Christ to a fearful and disoriented group of disciples, locked away in an upper room. Pope Leo XIV knew exactly what he was doing. He was inviting the Church—and the world—into the heart of Christ's message: peace, not as comfort but as a calling.

This peace, he emphasized, is not a fragile cease-fire or a temporary truce. It is the disarming peace of Christ—humble, persevering, unconditional. It is not imposed from above but sown from below. It does not begin in structures or speeches but in the heart of every person willing to live with open hands and an unguarded heart. For Pope Leo, peace is not merely a social value or political goal—it is the fruit of deep conversion, personal and communal.

Throughout his pastoral ministry, particularly as bishop of Chiclayo in Peru, Leo XIV lived this peace daily. In his diocesan writings, especially his reflections on Pope Francis' encyclical *Fratelli Tutti*, "On Fraternity and Social Friendship (2020), he laid out a vision of the Church as a field hospital and a bridge-builder in a fractured world. He invited people to rediscover fraternity as the pathway to peace, and listening as the method by which that peace is built. To speak of peace, he said, is to speak of transformation, reconciliation, and justice woven into daily life.

In a world wounded by war, division, and indifference, Pope Leo's approach to peace is radically evangelical. He does not deny conflict; he embraces it with the tools of the gospel. He rejects the language of "us versus them," instead calling for encounter, respect, and shared responsibility for the common good. His voice is calm but unwavering: "Evil will not prevail. We are all in God's hands."

For Leo XIV, *Fratelli Tutti* is not a text to be quoted but a path to be walked. He reads it not as a manifesto but as a spiritual itinerary. Peace is built not by policy alone but by the daily conversion of hearts. By seeking the suffering, welcoming the excluded, and healing the wounded, the Church becomes the living instrument of Christ's peace.

In his first blessing, *Urbi et Orbi*, Pope Leo XIV returned to this theme with piercing clarity. "The world needs his light. Humanity needs him as a bridge to be reached by God and his love." It is not enough, he insists, for the Church to speak of peace; it must live it, embody it, risk it. Peace is not soft. It is scandalous. It strips us of weapons—literal and emotional. It disarms our pride and prepares our hands for service.

And so, Pope Leo invites all—not just leaders or diplomats—to become artisans of peace. To begin in our families, our neighborhoods, our churches, and to believe, against all odds, that Christ's peace is possible. Because it is not our invention. It is his gift. And it is ours to give.

3.

God Loves Us Unconditionally

In a world shaped by performance, division, and worthiness, Pope Leo XIV's proclamation cuts through like light: "God loves us. God loves you all." These simple words, spoken in his first public message as pope, are not sentimental. They are foundational. They echo the heart of the gospel and reflect the deepest truth of Christian faith: that everything begins in the love of God.

For Pope Leo XIV, this is not only doctrine but also the starting point of everything the Church believes and does. Rooted in the teaching of St. Augustine, the Pope reminds us that love is not something we manufacture; it is something we receive. "We love," Augustine said, "because he first loved us."

God does not wait for us to be good before he loves us. He loves us into goodness. He embraces us while we are still far off. His love is freely given, faithful, and unconditional.

Leo XIV has lived this truth in the most pastoral of ways. During his years spent in Peru—especially through the trials of the pandemic—he wrote tenderly to his people. In a letter titled *Come and See...Let Us Come to Know Jesus Christ*, he insisted that faith is not about maintaining routines or sustaining structures. It is about returning to the heart of it all: the person of Jesus. We cannot proclaim what we have not encountered. And we cannot encounter Christ without being transformed by his love.

That encounter is not only for mystics or saints. It is for all. Christ comes to us personally, persistently, through his word, his presence, and his people. And for Pope Leo, this truth demands a response—not of fear, but of joy. The Church must not merely teach doctrine; it must communicate beauty. People are drawn not by obligation, but by attraction—by the radiant joy of knowing they are loved and welcomed by God.

Augustinian spirituality, which shaped Leo XIV from adolescence, emphasizes that truth is never imposed; it is discovered in community, in shared questions, in fraternal charity. That is why he insists that Christianity is not a private escape but a call to communion. God's love cannot be hoarded—it must be shared. "No one is disposable," he often repeats. "No one is a stranger in the eyes of Christ."

He invites the Church to become a space of encounter—a place where love is not just spoken; it is embodied. During his ministry, he urged communities to be "sowers of communion," especially during difficult times. The Christian life, he insists, is not an insurance policy for suffering but a mission born from love. To know we are loved is to be sent. The gospel is not preserved; it is proclaimed through lives that radiate this love.

Pope Leo is clear: this love does not exempt us from pain, but it transforms pain into revelation. Even in suffering, God draws near. Even in silence, God speaks. For Leo XIV, the Christian response to any crisis—whether global or personal—is to begin again in love. In the words of the psalm he often cites: "Your face, Lord, do I seek!" (Psalm 27:8).

This part of his message is not merely theological. It is deeply human. God's love is not a reward; it is the source. And once received, it sends us out to love without fear, to build community without judgment, and to walk with others in the joy of being loved first.

4.

Evil Will Not Prevail

"Evil will not prevail." With these four words, Pope Leo XIV announced not only his conviction but also the foundation of his hope. In a time when many hearts are overwhelmed by war, injustice, cynicism, and fear, he reminds us that evil—however loud or violent—does not have the final word. This is not blind optimism or rhetorical comfort. It is gospel truth rooted in the resurrection: Christ is risen, and his victory is sure.

Leo XIV does not deny the reality of evil. On the contrary, he names it plainly: inequality, migration crises, polarization, technological manipulation, environmental destruction, spiritual confusion, and dehumanization. But he does this not from a place of fear but from a place of faith. His is a prophetic voice, echoing the apostle Paul: "Do not be conquered by evil but conquer evil with good" (Romans 12:21). For Leo XIV, evil is real—but it is not ultimate. God is.

When he chose the name "Leo," he intentionally placed himself in the lineage of Pope Leo XIII, a pioneer of Catholic Social Teaching who faced the moral upheavals of the Industrial Age with gospel clarity. Now, in our own era of artificial intelligence, global conflict, and cultural fragmentation, Leo XIV responds with the same pastoral boldness: a Church that proclaims justice, promotes peace, and walks beside the poor. Evil will not prevail—not because of political victories, but because the cross and resurrection have already broken its power.

His words are not disconnected from life. Leo XIV has lived through suffering—his own and others'. As bishop of Chiclayo, he stood beside people wounded by violence and poverty. In homilies and letters, he reminded them: "We are all in God's hands." Not in the hands of fate, not in the grip of fear, but in the firm, faithful, compassionate hands of the

Father. This belief—anchored in prayer and pastoral experience—shapes his papacy.

He knows that faith is not a shield from pain but a light through it. In a homily recalling the prophet Elijah's despair, he said, "Even when we feel we can't go on, God comes and walks with us." Leo XIV constantly emphasizes the importance of community in facing evil. Alone, we may falter. But together, nourished by prayer and mutual support, we persevere. The Church, he says, is called to embody God's compassion—tenderness, not judgment, is our most urgent prophecy.

The phrase "do not be afraid," repeated often by Christ and echoed by Pope John Paul II, is central to Leo XIV's message. He repeats it now—not as a slogan but as an invitation. "Do not be afraid," he says to young people discerning their vocations, to families burdened by uncertainty, to communities facing persecution. God is with us. He never abandons his people.

To say "evil will not prevail" is not to minimize suffering. It is to remember the deeper truth: that Christ has overcome the world. This conviction empowers us to resist despair, to stand for truth, and to live with courage. It reminds us that perseverance is not naive—it is an act of faith.

Pope Leo XIV invites us to live from that conviction. To believe, again, that love is stronger than hatred, that light is more enduring than darkness, and that grace is at work—quietly but surely—in the world. "We are in God's hands," he says. And because of that, we can move forward. Without fear.

5.

Jesus the Good Shepherd

"I am the good shepherd. A good shepherd lays down his life for the sheep" (John 10:11). These words from John's Gospel were among the first that Pope Leo XIV proclaimed after his election. They were not chosen randomly. They express the core of his pastoral vision and spiritual identity. For Leo XIV, Jesus is not only the Teacher, not only the Savior—but, above all, the Good Shepherd: close, compassionate, faithful, and self-giving. And the Church, too, must be marked by this same heart.

From his early days as an Augustinian friar in Chicago to his missionary years in Peru, from seminary classrooms to remote mountain parishes, Pope Leo XIV has consistently lived this model of shepherding. He knows that to shepherd is not merely to lead. It is to accompany. It is to carry, to listen, to stay behind when someone is lost, and to move forward when others are afraid. The image of the shepherd is not sentimental for him—it is a rule of life.

This pastoral model shaped his entire episcopacy in Chiclayo. He visited isolated communities not for formality, but for friendship. He knew the names and stories of the people he served. He listened to catechists, walked with families, and ministered to priests with the same tenderness he had learned from the gospel. He reminded them that Jesus never abandons his flock, and we cannot abandon those entrusted to us.

For Leo XIV, the bishop is not a distant figure but is a father and a brother. He sees the episcopal ministry not as authority over others but as responsibility for them. He has spoken movingly of the bishop's crosier—the curved staff that symbolizes the duty to guide, support, and sometimes gently bring back those who wander. The bishop, he says, must walk in three places: ahead to lead, among to accompany, and behind to gather the weak. This is not his theory—this is his witness.

In Rome, when he served as prefect of the Dicastery for Bishops, Leo XIV brought this vision to a global scale. He looked for bishops who were not administrators but pastors. Men of communion, of humility, of gospel-centered leadership. Bishops who, as he said, "smell of the sheep," echoing Pope Francis. He resisted the temptation to see leadership as strategy, and he returned it to its roots: the image of Christ who lays down his life in love.

But this call is not only for clergy. Pope Leo XIV reminds all the baptized that we, too, are called to reflect the Good Shepherd. In our homes, workplaces, parishes, and neighborhoods, we are called to care for one another, to seek the lost, to carry burdens, and to love without counting the cost. Every Christian, in his or her own way, is invited to live with a shepherd's heart.

In a world that often feels leaderless, fragmented, and anxious, Leo XIV proposes a leadership of gentleness, courage, and proximity. Not power, but presence. Not control, but care. In this model, there is no room for arrogance, indifference, or harshness. There is only the steady rhythm of one who walks with others, guided by love.

The Church, he insists, must embody this shepherding spirit. It must be a home where the wounded are healed, where the fearful are consoled, and where all can hear the voice of the One Shepherd who knows them by name. This is the Church of Jesus. This is the Church Leo XIV seeks to lead.

6.

To Be Missionaries

"To proclaim the gospel, to be missionaries." These words, spoken by Pope Leo XIV at the beginning of his pontificate, are not a slogan or a program—they are his lived identity. From the moment he entered religious life as a young Augustinian, to the years he spent among the poor of Peru, to his current role as successor of Peter, Leo XIV has understood his vocation in one word: mission.

Mission, for him, is not something the Church *does*—it is who the Church *is*. Every baptized person, regardless of status or role, is called to be a missionary. That is not limited to far-off lands or dramatic gestures. It means bearing witness to the living Christ in one's everyday life—with courage, with compassion, and, above all, with joy. Pope

Leo has said again and again: the gospel is not an idea to be studied, but a person to be encountered and shared. Evangelization begins with relationship—with Christ and with others.

Leo XIV's own missionary journey began in earnest when, as a young friar, he was sent to the remote regions of northern Peru. There, in dusty towns and poor parishes, he learned the gospel all over again. He saw it in the resilience of the communities, in their love of Scripture, in their generosity despite lack, and in their hunger for justice. He did not bring Christ to Peru—he met Christ there. And he insists that this type of encounter shapes how we proclaim the gospel: not from superiority but from solidarity.

For Pope Leo XIV, mission is never just preaching. It is listening, healing, walking with people in their concrete reality. In his own words: "The Church's mission is not only to proclaim Christ but also to defend life, care for the poor, and protect the vulnerable." His understanding of mission includes human rights, social justice, ecological concern, and the defense of the dignity of every person. A Church that fails to speak up for the voiceless, he says, risks silencing the very gospel it preaches.

In a time when some prefer to retreat from the world, Leo XIV urges the Church to go out—to cross not only geographical borders but also the deeper boundaries of fear, indifference, and apathy. For him, the peripheries are not optional. They are privileged places of encounter. And those peripheries include not only the poor but also the forgotten, the doubting, the suffering, and the digitally isolated. Even the digital world, he notes, is a new mission territory—and one the Church must not fear to enter.

What drives this mission is not strategy, but love. Pope Leo echoes the early Church's kerygma: "Jesus Christ loves you, has given his life for you, and now lives at your side." That truth changes everything. And once one has experienced this love, one cannot help but share it.

Mission, then, is not a role for a few, but the task of all. To be missionary is to be Church. It is to live with eyes open to the needs of others, with hands ready to serve, and with hearts that burn with the desire for others to know Jesus. It is to say, as Pope Leo XIV does with quiet conviction, "Let us go forth. Without fear. With love."

7.

We Want to Be a Synodal Church

When Pope Leo XIV declares, "We want to be a synodal Church—a Church that walks together," he is not simply echoing a pastoral trend or repeating a catchphrase. He is articulating a vision of the Church that has shaped his entire ministry—from the remote parishes of Peru to the Vatican halls. For Leo XIV, synodality is not a project; it is a way of being. A way of listening to the Spirit, discerning together, and walking as one people of God.

The heart of synodality is communion. It is not about replacing hierarchy or structures but renewing them in the Spirit. Synodality invites every baptized person—lay, consecrated, or ordained—to take responsibility for the Church's life and mission. It calls us not to walk alone, nor to wait for someone else to speak, but to journey together in humility, listening deeply to God and to one another.

Leo XIV's formation in Augustinian spirituality has made him particularly attuned to this ecclesial vision. Saint Augustine's community life was built on shared discernment and mutual charity. That legacy flows through Leo XIV's understanding of synodality: not as endless debate but as a movement of the heart toward truth, shaped by prayer and guided by the Spirit. He often emphasizes that the first task in synodality is not talking—but listening. Listening to God. Listening to each other. Listening to the signs of the times.

During the global Synod on Synodality, Leo XIV—then Cardinal Prevost—described synodality as a "living experience of dialogue and discernment." He was clear: this is not just a new method, it is a conversion. It requires a shift in posture—from issuing statements to asking questions, from control to co-responsibility, from fear to trust. The

Spirit is not bound by the old ways. The Spirit, he says, "goes before us, overflows our expectations, and calls us to mutual listening."

In this synodal Church, bishops have a unique but not solitary role. They are not executives or judges; they are pastors who guide the people while remaining among them. Leo XIV has said that a bishop must be close to his people, not isolated. He must foster unity, not division. He must be a brother who listens, a servant who encourages, and a shepherd who walks alongside. This is the kind of leadership that heals wounds, builds trust, and allows the Church to move forward with integrity.

He also recognizes the temptations that threaten this journey—especially polarization. In the Church, as in society, it is easy to fall into camps, to label and dismiss, to reduce complexity to ideology. But Pope Leo is clear: the Church must resist this. Synodality is an antidote to polarization. It opens up space where people can be heard without being judged and where the Holy Spirit can surprise us with new paths of communion.

To live synodally is to journey with patience. It means allowing time for hearts to soften, for voices to be heard, for truths to emerge. It is not efficient—but it is faithful. It reflects the way Jesus walked with his disciples: asking questions, breaking bread, listening to fears, revealing the way forward gradually.

For Pope Leo XIV, this is not only a dream—it is a necessity. The Church of the twenty-first century cannot afford to work in silos or speak from pedestals. It must work—and walk—together, with the Spirit at the center. That is how the Church becomes what it is meant to be: a people on pilgrimage, united not by uniformity but by love.

8.

A United Church

"To walk with you, as a united Church." This phrase, spoken by Pope Leo XIV early in his pontificate, is more than a pastoral sentiment—it is a profound expression of his vision for the Church. In an age marked by fragmentation, ideological divisions, and ecclesial polarization, he offers a different path: unity rooted in Christ, nurtured in humility, and expressed in communion.

Unity is not about erasing difference, nor is it about blind agreement. For Pope Leo XIV, unity is the fruit of love—a love that embraces diversity without fear. Drawing from his Augustinian roots, he reminds the Church that unity is both gift and task. It is something we receive in Christ—"In the One, we are one"—but also something we must build every day through dialogue, forgiveness, and shared purpose.

His episcopal motto, *In Illo uno unum* ("In the One, we are one"), taken from Saint Augustine's commentary on the Psalms, has guided his ministry for decades. It is not merely decorative; it is a theological and pastoral commitment. He believes that communion is the deepest sign of the Church's credibility in the world. When Christians walk together, eat together, pray together, and discern together, they reveal the presence of Christ in their midst.

As bishop of Chiclayo, Leo XIV made unity the cornerstone of his ministry. He promoted participation among the laity, supported priests as brothers and co-workers, and encouraged synodal practices long before they became institutional priorities. He believed that the Eucharist was not just the "source and summit" of the Christian life, but also the beating heart of ecclesial unity. "Without the Eucharist," he once said, "there is no Church. And without communion, there is no credible gospel."

Unity, he teaches, is not uniformity. It is

not about everyone thinking alike, but about everyone being rooted in the same Spirit. It is a harmony born of shared faith and mutual love. In Rome, as prefect of the Dicastery for Bishops, he looked for leaders who could embody this unity—bishops who would not polarize but reconcile, not dominate but serve.

As Pope, Leo XIV continues this work with quiet determination. He calls the Church to reject divisive rhetoric and to heal the wounds of factionalism. He urges Catholics across the spectrum—traditional and progressive, conservative and reformist—to see each other not as enemies, but as brothers and sisters. Unity, he insists, does not weaken the Church. It is her strength.

He understands the cost of unity. It requires patience, forgiveness, and sometimes the humility to let go of being right. But the reward is great: a Church that breathes with both lungs, speaks with many voices, and walks with one heart.

In a world where difference so often leads to division, Pope Leo XIV offers a counter-witness. He shows us that unity is possible—not by force, but by grace. Not by silencing disagreement, but by listening through it. In a Church built on communion, the Spirit finds room to move, to surprise, and to renew.

And so, he invites us—bishops, priests, religious, and laypeople—to walk with him. Not behind him. With him. As a united Church. Rooted in Christ. Open to one another. Sent forth to the world as a sign of healing and hope.

9.

A Church That Builds Bridges

From the very beginning of his pontificate, Pope Leo XIV has been clear: the Church is not called to build walls but to build bridges. This conviction lies at the heart of his understanding of what it means to be a disciple of Christ in today's world. It's not about withdrawing into safe spaces or fortifying ecclesial identity against the modern age. Rather, it's about courageously stepping into the complexity of the world, encountering others, and forging paths of dialogue, reconciliation, and peace.

In his first public message, he spoke these words: "May you help us, and then help one another, to build bridges—through dialogue, through encounters—uniting all to be one people, always in peace." These were not diplomatic remarks. They were a roadmap for his pontificate. He envisions a Church that serves as a living bridge—between generations, between cultures, between those inside the Church and those far outside of it. A Church that is not afraid of questions, tensions, or wounds, but that steps into them with love.

Pope Leo XIV has seen the power of such bridge-building firsthand. As bishop of Chiclayo, he ministered in contexts marked by social unrest, economic hardship, and historical divisions. He witnessed how the Church can become a space of encounter—where political enemies speak to one another, where the poor are heard, where the suffering find comfort, and where the gospel opens space for healing. This vision grew not in theory, but in real streets and real communities.

To build bridges is not to compromise truth. On the contrary, it is to allow truth to do what it was always meant to do: bring people together. Pope Leo insists that the gospel cannot be preached in a spirit of antagonism. Truth is not a weapon—it is a gift. And the

Christian does not impose it; he proposes it, shares it, lives it.

This bridge-building includes ecumenical and interreligious dialogue. For Leo XIV, these are not political gestures or superficial pleasantries. They are expressions of the gospel's universal reach. All people are created in the image of God. All long for dignity, meaning, and peace. The Church, he says, must be the first to take the risk of crossing lines, meeting the other, and embracing shared humanity.

To build bridges also means healing divisions within the Church. Pope Leo knows the pain caused by polarization—where Catholics talk past each other or treat one another as threats. He refuses to reduce people to labels. Instead, he calls for a Church where different sensibilities can live together, not in conflict, but in communion. "Recognize one another as brothers and sisters," he says, not as opponents.

He often returns to the image of Jesus—whose entire mission was bridge-building: between heaven and earth, between God and humanity, between sinner and grace. The

Cross itself is the ultimate bridge: vertical in its communion with the Father, horizontal in its embrace of humanity. That is the model Leo XIV offers to the Church today.

This is not easy work. Bridge-building requires humility, patience, and the willingness to be misunderstood. But it is the most urgent task of the Church in a divided world. Pope Leo XIV calls the Church to be what it truly is: a sign of God's desire to draw all people to himself, across every divide. And he calls each of us to take up the mission—not with fear, but with open hearts.

10.

Mary Walks With Us

In the early moments of his pontificate, Pope Leo XIV knelt before an image of the Virgin Mary in silent prayer. There were no microphones, no announcements—only a gesture. Yet that quiet act spoke volumes. It revealed something profoundly personal and deeply theological: Mary is not just a figure in the background of the Church's story—she walks with us. For Pope Leo XIV, Mary is not distant, idealized, or inaccessible. She is close. She is Mother.

From his Augustinian formation, Leo XIV inherited a Marian spirituality that emphasizes both contemplation and action. Mary is the woman who listens, who ponders, and who acts. She is not passive. She is attentive. And she is deeply present in the life of every believer and every community.

"Our Mother Mary," he says, "always wants to walk with us." This is not poetry—it is conviction. It is experience. Mary accompanies the Church as she accompanied her Son: silently, faithfully, and with courage.

As bishop of Chiclayo, Pope Leo was profoundly influenced by the popular Marian devotion of the Peruvian people. In the remote villages where he served, Mary was not merely a doctrinal figure—she was family. She was called upon in times of joy and distress, honored in feast days and processions, invoked in every prayer. He saw in their devotion something that theology alone could not teach: Mary is not an abstract ideal, but a real companion.

In his pastoral letters and messages, he often spoke of Mary as the first disciple—the one who teaches us how to listen to God's voice, how to say "yes" to his call, how to remain faithful even in darkness. He described her not as a queen on a pedestal, but as a woman who walks beside us, who takes us by the hand when the road is hard, and who shows us how to follow Christ with trust.

For Pope Leo XIV, Mary also embodies

the Church's synodal spirit. She is the one who listens before she speaks, who treasures words in her heart before acting. She does not impose, but accompanies. She is present at every key moment in salvation history—from the Annunciation to Pentecost—not as a spectator, but as a protagonist. This Marian style is what Pope Leo desires for the Church: a community that discerns, listens, walks together, and remains close to the suffering.

Mary is also the model of missionary discipleship. After the Annunciation, she does not stay in Nazareth to contemplate her privilege. She sets out "in haste" to visit Elizabeth. She brings Christ with her. Pope Leo frequently draws on this image to remind the Church that true devotion leads to action. Marian spirituality is not retreat—it is readiness. To walk with Mary is to walk toward others, bearing Christ.

He also sees Mary as a source of comfort and strength in turbulent times. When the world trembles under the weight of conflict and uncertainty, Mary stands at the foot of the Cross and teaches us how to hope. In his own personal journey—from his calling in

Chicago to his missionary work in Peru to the Chair of Peter—Leo XIV has found in her a companion, an intercessor, and a model.

To entrust ourselves to Mary, he says, is not to escape reality—it is to enter it with grace. In her presence, we find room to breathe, space to trust, and strength to begin again. And so, Pope Leo XIV places his pontificate under her mantle—not as ornament, but as protection. Not as symbol, but as direction.

Mary walks with us. And where she walks, Christ is never far.

CONCLUSION

A Pontificate with Roots and a Future

Pope Leo XIV has not come to inaugurate a new ideology or to dismantle tradition. Rather, his pontificate emerges as a continuation of the gospel—lived faithfully in the footsteps of the Church's rich heritage, yet deeply attuned to the signs of our time. With the humility of a servant and the heart of a missionary, Leo XIV offers the Church a style of leadership that is pastoral, synodal, and profoundly evangelical. He leads not by command, but by communion. Not from above, but from within.

In these opening days of his papacy, the themes that have already surfaced reveal the contours of a Church that is both rooted and forward-looking. From his first message—

"Peace be with you"—to his firm assurance that "Evil will not prevail," to his quiet gesture of entrusting everything to Mary, Leo XIV has begun his mission not with force, but with faith. A faith shaped by the dusty roads of northern Peru, by the spiritual discipline of Augustinian community life, and by years of listening, discerning, and accompanying.

This is a pope who embodies what he preaches. He is not a distant theologian or a detached bureaucrat. He is a shepherd who has walked among his people, who knows what it means to lead with tears, to celebrate with the poor, and to break bread with those at the margins. His authority is not built on image or strategy, but on experience—deeply human, deeply spiritual.

Throughout this booklet, we've traced ten essential things Pope Leo XIV wants the Church to know. Each one reflects not just his theology, but his lived conviction. That God's love is the beginning of everything. That peace is the fruit of courage and humility. That the Church must build bridges, not walls. That the path forward is synodal—

walked together, guided by the Spirit. That Mary walks with us still.

He does not shy away from the challenges the Church faces: polarization, secularization, ecological crisis, technological upheaval, and global inequality. But neither does he meet these challenges with fear. His is a steady, hopeful voice—a voice that reminds us that Christ remains at the center, and that the gospel is still good news.

In many ways, Pope Leo XIV represents the convergence of two great traditions: the intellectual and communal depth of the Augustinian heritage, and the missionary and pastoral energy of the Latin American Church. He brings both to bear on the global stage with gentle clarity. He does not offer spectacle—but depth. He does not seek applause—but transformation.

And he calls each of us—not just leaders and theologians, but all the baptized—to walk with him. To live our faith not as ritual obligation, but as joyful witness. To return to Christ. To seek the face of God in the face of the poor. To be the Church the world longs to see: merciful, just, united, and brave.

With roots firmly planted in the tradition and eyes fixed on Christ, Pope Leo XIV is a pope for this moment—and for the journey ahead. His words echo the wisdom of his spiritual father, Saint Augustine: "Let love be rooted in you, and from that root, nothing but good can grow."

That is his hope. That is his promise. That is the path he invites us to follow.